TABLE OF CONTENTS

Chapter 1	The Baptist Church– A Denomination.	1
	What is a Denomination?	2
	What does the Bible Say about Denominations?	3
	Denominationalism Compared to New Testament Christianity	4
Chapter 2	Baptism.	9
	The Candidate for Baptism	10
	In Christ	16
	Baptism is Necessary for Church Membership, but not for Salvation?	19
	What if a Person Wants to be Baptized, but Dies Before He or She has an Opportunity?	21
	Is Baptism a "Work"?	22
	What about Paul's Statement, "Christ Sent Me not to Baptize"?	26
	Is Salvation the Result of "Baptismal Regeneration"?	30
	What about the Thief on the Cross?	32
	Don't Some Baptist Churches Teach that Baptism is Essential for Salvation?	36

	When Should a Person be Re-baptized?. 37
	How Important is the Doctrine of Baptism? 41
Chapter 3	The Perseverance of the Saints 43
Chapter 4	Church Organization 59
Chapter 5	Conclusion 65
Appendix A	"Calling on the name of the Lord". . 69
Appendix B	Holy Spirit Baptism 77
References	 85

Special thanks to Eric Lyons and Dave Miller, who graciously allowed the author to use portions of their works throughout the book and especially in the two appendices.

What the Bible says about the Baptist Church

Kyle Butt, M.A.

Apologetics Press, Inc.
230 Landmark Drive
Montgomery, Alabama 36117-2752

© Copyright 2007
ISBN: 978-0-932859-82-2

All rights reserved. No part of this book may be reproduced in any form without permission from the publisher, except in the case of brief quotations.
All Scripture quotations are from The New King James Version of the Bible, unless otherwise specified. Copyright © 1982, Thomas Nelson, Inc.

Library of Congress Cataloging-in-Publication
Kyle Butt, 1976 -
  What the Bible says about the Baptist Church/Kyle Butt
  Includes bibliographic references
  ISBN: 978-0-932859-82-2
  1. Comparative religion. 2. Christian theology. I. Title

280—dc22   2005926365

Introduction

It is with a heavy heart that I survey the religious scene of America in the 21st century. Approximately 140 million Americans claim some type of religious affiliation with over 140 different religious groups, the largest of those groups being the Catholic Church with about 62 million adherents, and the second largest being the Southern Baptist denomination with 20 million members. I presently live in Montgomery, Alabama, but I spent most of my formative years in the mountains of east Tennessee and the rolling hills of middle Tennessee. Since these two states combined claim over 2.5 million Southern Baptists, it is no wonder that several of the influential people in my life have been members of the Baptist denomination. I sat by Baptists in school, passed a basketball to my Baptist teammates on Friday nights, and ate lunch with my Baptist friends throughout the week. The truth is, of all the people and groups of people with whom I have come in contact throughout the world, as a whole, Baptists are some of the most sincere, highly moral people that I have encountered.

It is because of that sincerity and morality that this book has been written. In the *Baptist Faith and Message*, the denomination states its straightforward belief that "the Holy Bible was written by men divinely inspired and is God's revelation of Himself to man. It is a perfect treasure of divine instruction. It has God for its author, salvation for its end, and truth, without any mixture of error, for its matter" (2000, Article I, p. 7). The Baptist denomination claims to set the Bible as its standard of law and instruction. It will be the purpose of this book to investigate the truth of that claim. Because the Baptist denomination is bound by no formal creed, and because each congregation is autonomous, the majority of this book will simply lay the Scriptures beside what the Baptist denomination teaches in a sincere effort to compare the two.

With approximately 27 divisions of the Baptist Church, including Southern Baptist, Free Will Baptist, Landmark Baptist, etc., it is difficult to determine exactly what each division teaches. However, several tenets of Baptist doctrine are held in common by most Baptists. This book will deal with only a few of those major tenets. And, since the Southern Baptist denomination is the largest Baptist division, many of the references documenting Baptist teaching come from its leaders.

It is my earnest desire that those Baptists who read this book will heed the words of one of their founding fathers. In 1609, John Smyth, in defending his position to change religions, wrote: "To change a false Religion is commendable, and to retain a false Religion is damnable" (as quoted in McBeth, 1990, p. 19). I have written this book out of love, in order to speak directly to individual Baptists who have sincere hearts and who want to know the Truth.

Chapter 1

THE BAPTIST CHURCH— A DENOMINATION

Most religious people in the United States are quite familiar with the word "denomination." In fact, multiplied millions of people all over the world are members of one religious denomination or another. The Baptist Church, without hesitation, identifies itself as a Christian denomination. James Sullivan, in his book, *Baptist Polity: As I See It,* wrote an entire chapter titled "Typical Kinds of Denominational Structures." In that chapter he repeatedly discussed the Southern Baptist **denomination** (1998, pp. 45-58). In the *Baptist Faith and Message*, under Article XIV titled "Cooperation," the text states: "cooperation is desirable between the various Christian **denominations**" (emp. added). In 2001, Albert Mohler Jr., then-president of the Southern Baptist Theological Seminary, described the Baptist Church as a "denomination" at least four times in his three-page introduction to Stanton Norman's book, *More Than Just a Name* (2001a, pp. vii-ix). Further reading of most Baptist literature could multiply these types of quotes by the hundreds. Therefore, we must ask, "What is a denomination?" and, "What does the Bible say about denominations?"

What is a Denomination?

Consider the following dictionary definitions (*American...*, 2000, p. 485). The term "denominate" means "to give a name to; designate." A "Denomination" is a "large group of religious congregations united under a common faith and name and organized under a single administrative and legal hierarchy; a name or designation, especially for a class or group." The term "denominator" refers to the "expression written below the line in a common fraction that indicates the number of parts into which one whole is divided." "Denominationalism" is the "tendency to separate into religious denominations; sectarianism." Think about these meanings for just a moment. The very word "denomination" means a named or designated division. Denominationalism occurs when religious people and groups divide and segregate themselves on the basis of different designations or church affiliations and different doctrines.

What does the Bible Say about Denominations?

Edward Hiscox wrote *The Standard Manual for Baptist Churches*. By 1951, at least 160,000 of his manuals were in print. In his section titled "Church-membership," he wrote: "It is most likely that in the Apostolic age when there was but 'one Lord, one faith, and one baptism,' and **no differing denominations** existed, the baptism of a convert by the very act constituted him a member of the church" (1903, p. 22, emp. added). Herschel Hobbs, in his book, *What Baptists Believe,* wrote: "The word 'church' is never used in the New Testament in the sense of a denomination or of any segment of organized historic Christianity." Two pages later, he again stated: "The word 'church' is never used in the New Testament to refer to a building or a denomination. It is used only to refer to all the redeemed of all ages and to a local body of baptized believers. The majority of its references are to the local church" (1964, pp. 75, 77). Ernest Mosley, in *Basics for Baptists*, declared:

> The word *church* in the New Testament is never used to refer to a building—"Our church is south of town on Highway 29"; an activity—"Are you going to 11:00 a.m. church tomorrow?"; **or a denomination**—"I always thought you were a member of the Methodist church." **It refers either to the redeemed in Christ of all the ages or to a local body (congregation) of believers in Christ**..." (1996, p. 55, emp. added).

By looking at these quotes from several Baptist authorities, it is clear they recognized that the Lord's church in the New Testament was not described by the inspired writers as a denomination.

In fact, the idea of Christianity being split into various divisions or denominations goes against the concepts found in the New Testament. Paul made this point to the church in Corinth: "I beseech you brothers by the name of our Lord Jesus Christ that you all speak the same thing and that there be no divisions among you" (1 Corinthians 1:10). Here is a passage that says divisions are not supposed to exist. "Let there be no divisions among you." If a denomination is a "designated division," then denominationalism is clearly against the will of Christ (John 17:20-21). The passage continues, "but that you be perfectly joined together in the same mind and in the same judgment." It is clear when we go to the Bible that denominationalism, though viewed innocently by millions of people worldwide, is an approach to religion that is out of harmony with New Testament teaching.

Denominationalism Compared to New Testament Christianity

Consider New Testament teaching on the subject of the one church. In Matthew 16:18, Jesus said: "Upon this rock I will build my church." In Colossians 1:13, Paul spoke of Christians as those who had been removed by God from darkness and translated into the kingdom of

His dear Son. In Ephesians 1:22-23, the body of Christ is referred to as the church, and later we are told that there is only **one** (4:4). That body is the church of our Lord. He established it; He built it; He purchased it with His own blood (Acts 20:28). If there is only one church, then God cannot be pleased with the division of competing churches with various names, doctrines, and practices. In 1 Corinthians 1:12, Paul wrote concerning such division: "Now I say this, that each of you says, 'I am of Paul,' or 'I am of Apollos,' or 'I am of Cephas,' or 'I am of Christ.' Is Christ divided? Was Paul crucified for you? Or were you baptized in the name of Paul?" The various members of the Corinthian church were dividing themselves along the lines of who they thought the most influential leaders were. Paul confronted and rebuked this idea of division.

Furthermore, we find clearly depicted on the pages of the New Testament the idea of scriptural names for Christ's church, that is, names for both the church itself and names for individual members of that church. In Romans 16:16, we find the expression "churches of Christ." In 1 Corinthians 1:2, we have a reference to "the church of God." In 1 Corinthians 3:16, we find "the temple of God." And in Ephesians 4:12, we have the phrase "the body of Christ."

These expressions are not intended to be technical nor formal names for the church. They are descriptions. They are labels that describe Christ's church. Additional ones may be found as well. Most of the time in the New Testament, Christ's church is referred to simply as "the church." But here is the point: most of the names that people attach to denominations today are not used in the New Testament to describe the Lord's church. In the New Testament, the Lord's body or church is never called the Baptist Church.

The same thing is true with regard to the names that God wants individual Christians to wear. In the New Testament, we read that followers of Christ were called Christians (Acts 11:26). In Romans 1:7, we find the term "saints," and in Acts 5:14, we find the term "believer" applied to Christ's followers. In other passages, we find the word "disciple," or familial names like "brother" and the "family of God." Yet, we never read of a person being called a Pauline Christian, or an Apollonian Christian, nor do we read that any Christian was ever called a Lutheran, Presbyterian, or Baptist Christian. Does it not cast doubt on the legitimacy of a denomination when the names it uses are not names used in the New Testament for either the Lord's church or individual Christians?

New Testament truth on the matter of names is simple. While it is true that some denominations have taken the names of men and applied them to themselves and their churches (e.g., Lutheran), and other churches designate themselves by a particular practice or doctrine (e.g., Presbyterian, Baptist, Episcopalian), such practices are not sanctioned in the Bible. To be accurate and acceptable to God, we should be only Christians and Christians only, having no other names than those that are biblical, and being members of no denomination, but simply members of Christ's church.

Chapter 2

BAPTISM

It is here that we come to one of the most fundamental beliefs of the Baptist church—baptism. When studying the denomination as a whole, a generally accepted notion of baptism is easy to discern. First, Baptists correctly believe that New Testament baptism consists of total immersion in water. Herschel Hobbs correctly summed up the view of the Baptist church in this regard in his book *What Baptists Believe*: "Baptism in the New Testament is never by sprinkling or pouring" (1964, p. 83). J. Newton Brown, in his work, *A Baptist Church Manual*, wrote: "We believe that Christian baptism is the immersion in water of a believer..." (1994, p. 24). And Article 7 of the *Baptist Faith and Message* states: "Christian baptism is the immersion of a believer in water..." (2000, p. 14). This belief of total immersion in water is justified and demanded by the New Testament text. In fact, the Greek word *baptidzo,* from which we get our English word "baptize," means to "dip, immerse, plunge, or sink" (Arndt, et al., 1979, p. 131). Practices such as sprinkling or pouring are rightly rejected by the Baptist denomination due to the lack of biblical support for such techniques.

The Candidate for Baptism

Who is eligible to be baptized, according to the Baptist denomination? Baptists firmly believe that only persons who are old enough and mature enough to believe in Christ should be baptized. Hobbs summed up the generally held belief: "The New Testament knows nothing of infant baptism but that of believers only" (1964, p. 83). Albert Mohler Jr. wrote: "Our rejection of infant baptism is rooted in the clear normative New Testament witness to the baptism of believers by immersion" (2001, p. 63). Here again, the Baptist denomination has held firmly to the New Testament example of baptizing only those individuals who have the maturity and intelligence to indicate their personal belief in Jesus. The Baptist denomination is right to insist that infant baptism is an unauthorized practice, since every New Testament example of baptism portrays a mature individual who believes in Christ.

Other criteria are used by the Baptist denomination to assess whether they feel that a person is eligible for baptism. According to those in the Baptist denomination, a person must prove that he or she has already been saved by God through some type of saving experience before baptism. The following quotes from Baptist authorities and documents testify to this fact. Fred Malone, in his contribution to the book, *Why I Am A Baptist,* wrote that "candidates for baptism should have an adequate understanding of the person and work of Jesus Christ and the gospel of repentance and faith... This requires that the faith **and salvation experience of an individual must be examined before baptism**" (2001, p. 139, emp. added). In the same book, Donna Ascol made the following statement: "I am convinced by Scripture that only those who are saved by God's grace are scriptural candidates for baptism" (p. 158). She further defined her position, in words more familiar to the general Baptist adherent, when she commented: "Baptism, in the New Testament, is an external sign of an internal work of grace already attained in the heart of the believer" (p. 159). As Hobbs further noted: "Regeneration is an act of God, not man (John 1:13). Since it is by grace, it obviously cannot be produced, aided, or completed by baptism. **Baptism is the symbol of the experience, not its source or means** (Rom. 6:4-5)" (1964, p. 99, emp. added).

With this point of Baptist doctrine, the New Testament does not agree. As will be shown in the next several pages, no person in the New Testament was ever asked to produce proof that he or she was already saved **before** being baptized. In fact, the New Testament insists that during baptism, a person comes in contact with the blood of Christ, and it is at that point that his or her sins are forgiven—not before.

There is no question about **what** forgives a person's sins. The New Testament is unambiguous in its claim that only the blood of Jesus can forgive sins. Hebrews 9:22 states that "without shedding of blood there is no remission." Ephesians 1:7 declares: "In Him [Christ—KB] we have redemption through His blood, the forgiveness of sins, according to the riches of His grace." Speaking about Jesus Christ, John wrote: "To Him who loved us and washed us from our sins in His own blood" (Revelation 1:5). The Hebrews writer further commented: "Therefore Jesus also, that He might sanctify the people with His own blood, suffered outside the gate" (Hebrews 13:12). The Baptist denomination correctly identifies the blood of Jesus as the only thing with the power to forgive sins.

However, the denomination incorrectly identifies **when** a person comes in contact with that blood. According to the Baptist denomination, a person is forgiven when he or she repents and "accepts Jesus into" his or her heart. In his article titled "Baptist on the Hot Seat," Tom Elliff told of his "conversion" in these words.

> Late on Thursday evening, after waiting for my father to come home from the crusade, I knelt with both my parents, repented of sin, and trusted Christ. I could (and I still can!) remember the incredible

sense of peace that flooded my heart.... I was not baptized until the following fall, after my father assumed the pastorate of the Bethany Baptist Church in Kansas City, Missouri (2001, p. 131).

In relating his father's "conversion experience" in his book, *Foundations of the Faith: The Doctrines Baptists Believe*, Roy T. Edgemon wrote: "Suddenly, my dad's spiritual blindness was gone, and he saw the truth of salvation. He prayed, 'God, forgive me and save me.' **Salvation came at that moment of acceptance**. When Dad accepted Christ and let Christ do the saving, he was saved" (1999, p. 72, emp. added). This view, that a person's sins are forgiven when he or she "asks Jesus into his heart," or when a person prays the "sinner's prayer," is almost universally held among Baptists. Billy Graham, arguably the most famous Southern Baptist evangelist of all time, wrote: "To receive Christ you need to do four things: (1) Admit your spiritual need. 'I am a sinner'; (2) repent and be willing to turn from your sin; (3) believe that Jesus Christ died for you on the cross; (4) receive, through prayer, Jesus Christ into your heart and life" (1996, p. 11).

Mosley, in his work, *Basics for Baptists*, wrote: "Although some Christian denominations believe that salvation is either begun or completed in the act of baptism, Baptists believe that salvation occurs when a person repents of sin and trusts Jesus Christ to be Savior and Lord of his or her life" (1996, p. 25). Therefore, Baptists believe and teach that a person comes in contact with the blood of Christ **when** that person "accepts Jesus into his heart as his savior" or prays the "sinner's prayer."

Yet, the Bible disagrees with this Baptist doctrine that lies at the foundation of the denomination. According to the New Testament, a person contacts the blood of Christ only in the waters of baptism. The apostle Paul wrote: "Or do you not know that as many of us as were baptized into Christ Jesus were baptized into his death?" (Romans 6:3). In Christ's death, His blood was shed. Paul is stating that baptism is the point **when** a person contacts the blood of Christ. In Acts 2:38, after the Jews asked Peter what they needed to do to remove their guilt, Peter said: "Repent, and let every one of you be baptized in the name of Jesus Christ for the remission of sins." If Paul, in Ephesians 1:7, stated that in Christ we have forgiveness of sins through the blood of Jesus, and if Peter told the Jews on Pentecost to repent and be baptized "for the forgiveness of sins," then **when** did the apostles teach that a person contacts the blood of Christ? In the waters of baptism. Peter further clarified his position on baptism in 1 Peter 3:21, wherein he stated: "There is also an antitype which now saves us, namely baptism (not the removal of the filth of the flesh, but the answer of a good conscience toward God), through the resurrection of Jesus Christ." Peter did not mean that baptism saves a person apart from the blood of Jesus. He simply was saying that a person contacts the blood of Jesus **when** that person is baptized.

When Nicodemus came to Christ at night to discuss matters of salvation, Jesus Himself contended: "Most assuredly, I say to you, unless one is born of water and the Spirit, he cannot enter the kingdom of God." Jesus' statement, "born of water," has given Baptist writers difficult problems over the years. Hobbs wrote concerning this passage:

> An analysis of John 3 suggests the issue to be a contrast between the natural and the spiritual birth (cf. vv. 3-7). Nicodemus thought of the natural birth; Jesus spoke of the spiritual birth. "Born of water" refers not to baptism but to the water birth or that which accompanies the natural birth. So Jesus says before one can be born again (spiritual) he must be born for the first time (natural) (1964, p. 99).

Hobbs' analysis of John 3 fails on several accounts. First, why would Jesus say that a person has to be born **physically** before He can be born spiritually? That is a truism that Nicodemus would have understood from the beginning of the discussion. Does Hobbs mean to suggest that Nicodemus thought a person could get to heaven without having a physical existence? Hobbs' definition of "water" in this case makes Jesus' statement meaningless. Second, the discussion between Jesus and Nicodemus comes only a few verses before John 3: 22-23, which reads: "After these things Jesus and His disciples came into the land of Judea, and there He remained with them and baptized. Now John also was baptizing in Aenon near Salim, because there was much water there." Jesus' comment about being "born of water" is set in the general context of baptism in the same chapter. Third, if the word "water" in Jesus' phrase, "born of water," means "that which accompanies the natural birth," then why doesn't the word retain the same meaning throughout the chapter? What, then, are we to do with verse 23, which declares that "there was much water there"?

In Christ

Another way to find out **when** a person comes into contact with the blood of Christ is to examine the phrase "**in Christ**" in the New Testament. Depending on what version you read, the phrase is used approximately 80 different times. What do we find "in Christ?" Paul, in the book of Ephesians, used the phrase multiple times in chapter 1. He stated that "every spiritual blessing" is found **in Christ** (Ephesians 1:3). He also stated that "forgiveness of sins" is found only **in Christ** (vs. 7). In the book of Romans, He further stated that "redemption" (Romans 3:24) and "eternal life" (Romans 6:23) are located **in Christ**. The inspired Paul told the young man Timothy that "salvation" is **in Christ** (2 Timothy 2:10). Paul obviously wanted his readers to understand that everything good in the spiritual realm is found in Christ alone. When discussing things outside of Christ, Paul painted a grim picture of a place without hope and without God (Ephesians 2:12).

After looking at the phrase "in Christ," the question arises: How does a person get into Christ? It is interesting to note that the New Testament specifically mentions water baptism as one essential element that puts a person into Christ. Romans 6:3 states: "Or do you not know that as many of us as **were baptized into Christ Jesus** were baptized into His death?" (emp added). And Galatians 3:27 declares: "For as many of you as **were baptized into Christ** have put on Christ" (emp. added). While some have incorrectly attempted to claim that the baptism mentioned in these two verses refers to Holy Spirit baptism (see Appendix B), the Baptist denomination as a whole does not resort to this faulty line of reasoning. In fact, Baptists often use Romans 6:3 and Galatians 3:27 to support their insistence upon the necessity of water baptism.

Andrew Davis, in his contribution to the book, *Why I Am A Baptist,* wrote that water baptism "was commanded by Christ in the Great Commission (Matt. 28:19) and demonstrates the new life in Christ for every disciple (Rom. 6)" (2001, p. 118). His clear reference to Romans 6 shows that he understands water baptism is under discussion in that chapter. Hobbs, in *What Baptists Believe*, wrote: "Baptism is the symbol of the experience, not its source or means (Rom. 6:4-5)" (1964, p.

99). Once again, these references to Romans chapter six by authorities on Baptist doctrine verify that the Baptist denomination understands Paul to be discussing water baptism in Romans 6:3.

The Baptist preacher Conrad Mbewe wrote: "I also saw that baptism signified dying with Christ, being buried with him, and rising together with him in newness of life (Romans 6:4). It was an outward physical expression of an inward spiritual experience" (2001, p. 97). In regard to the second passage, Galatians 3:27, Baptists are equally insistent upon this verse's application to water baptism. J. Newton Brown, in his work, *A Baptist Church Manual,* listed both Romans 6:4 and Galatians 3:27-28 in his section discussing water baptism as taught in the New Testament (1994, pp. 23-24). Roy T. Edgemon, in *Foundations of the Faith: The Doctrines Baptists Believe*, commented on this passage in a section dealing with water baptism, saying:

> Baptism is a picture; in fact, it is several pictures. First, it pictures the death, burial, and resurrection of Christ. Second, it pictures the believer's death to sin and resurrection to new life in Christ. Third, it pictures union with Christ; immersion in the name of the Triune God indicates a new life in Christ (see Romans 6:4; Galatians 3:27) [1999, p. 98].

It is clear from the Baptist writers themselves that the denomination as a whole considers Galatians 3:27 and Romans 6:3-4 to be discussing **water** baptism.

Let us, then, put these pieces together. If the Bible says that forgiveness and all spiritual blessings are in Christ, and if Romans 6:3 and Galatians 3:27 clearly state that water baptism is the point at which a person gets into Christ, then any accountable person who has not been baptized by water is outside of Christ. The water of baptism does not save anyone, but it is the point at which a person contacts the saving blood of Christ.

It is ironic that the Baptist denomination teaches that Romans 6:3 and Galatians 3:27 talk about water baptism, yet at the same time deny that water baptism puts a person into Christ. Unfortunately for the Baptist denomination, such a belief militates against the straightforward reading of these two passages, which show that water baptism is the point **when** a person contacts the saving blood of Christ.

Baptism is Necessary for Church Membership, but not for Salvation?

From reading Baptist material, it is easy to see that only baptized individuals are granted membership in any Baptist church. Stan Norman, writing in *Why I Am a Baptist?*, commented: "Although insisting that baptism is unnecessary for salvation, Baptists contend that it is important and necessary for church membership" (2001b, p. 185). In another 2001 book published by Broadman and Holman (one of the most well-known Baptist publishing companies), Norman said: "Baptist churches follow biblical teachings when they allow only immersed person into their memberships." And again, "Baptism is also a necessary requirement for church membership" (2001a, pp. 102,104). Speaking conclusively on this fundamental Baptist doctrine, the *Baptist Faith and Message* commented: "Christian baptism is the immersion of a believer in water in the name of the Father, the Son, and the Holy Spirit.... Being a church ordinance, it is prerequisite to the privileges of church membership and to the Lord's Supper" (2000, p. 14). We see, then, that in order to be a member of any Baptist church, a person must be baptized.

Baptists insist, however, that baptism is not essential to a person's salvation. Ascol summed up the Baptist view on baptism when she stated: "It is not essential for salvation" (2001, p. 159). Are we to understand that a person can be a member of the Lord's church without being baptized, but can be a member of a Baptist church only after baptism? And, if a person can be a member of the Lord's saved without being baptized, then that would mean that the Baptist denomination is not the Lord's church. In truth, it is through baptism that a person contacts the blood of Christ. And no one can be saved without coming in contact with that blood through water baptism.

Baptism

What if a Person Wants to be Baptized, but Dies Before He or She has an Opportunity?

One of the most frequently used arguments against the necessity of baptism for salvation is the idea that "God would not do that." The question is asked, "What if a sincere believing person is on his way to be baptized and dies right before he gets to the water? Are you telling me that God would send that person to hell just because he did not make it to the water?" At first glance, this argument may seem legitimate. Upon further investigation, however, it is easy to see that it is a simple play on emotions, and in no way disproves the necessity of baptism for salvation.

The "God-would-not-do-that" argument can be used against almost any commandment in the Bible. For instance, the Bible repeatedly says that a person must believe that Jesus is the Son of God (Romans 10:11; John 8:24; et al.). Suppose, then, that a Christian had just begun to tell the story of Jesus to an older gentleman, when suddenly that gentleman had a massive heart attack and died without getting to hear the rest of the story, and thus did not have the opportunity to believe. Should we, therefore, do away with the biblical command to believe in Jesus Christ, simply because a theoretical scenario can be concocted in which a potential convert dies moments before his compliance? To ask is to answer. Nor, with a wave of the hand, can we do away with the biblical command to be baptized for the forgiveness of sins.

Consider the fact that the Bible plainly states that God wants all people to be saved. In 2 Peter 3:9, the inspired apostle wrote: "The Lord is not slack concerning His promise, as some count slackness, but is longsuffering toward us, not willing that any should perish but that all should come to repentance." The Old Testament prophet Ezekiel was instructed by God to convey this message to the Israelites on God's behalf: "'As I live,' says the Lord God, 'I have no pleasure in the death of the wicked, but that the wicked turn from his way and live'" (Ezekiel 33:11). The apostle Paul told the young preacher Timothy that God "desires all men to be saved and to come to the knowledge of the truth" (1 Timothy 2:3-4). Therefore, if a person truly and honestly wants to become a Christian by being baptized for the forgiveness of his sins as God commanded, then God (Who wants all to be saved and is watchful of each individual human) certainly would provide an opportunity for that person to obey His commandment to be baptized.

Is Baptism a "Work"?

The idea that water baptism is necessary for salvation is sometimes questioned, based upon the assumption that baptism is a work of human merit that is supposed to "earn" a person's salvation. According to this line of reasoning, salvation cannot come **after** baptism, because baptism is a "work" and the apostle Paul wrote: "For by grace you have been saved through faith, and that not of yourselves; it is the gift of God, **not of works**, lest anyone should boast" (Ephesians 2:8-9, emp. added).

Once again, however, several points make it clear that the necessity of water baptism cannot be dismissed using this argument. First, it is evident from the New Testament that there are certain things that a person must do in order to be saved. The Baptist denomination accepts the idea that a person cannot be saved without first believing in Jesus Christ. In the *Baptist Faith and Message*, the text under Article IV, paragraph A, states: "Repentance and faith are inseparable experiences of grace. Repentance is a genuine turning from sin toward God. Faith is the acceptance of Jesus Christ and commitment of the entire personality to Him as Lord and Saviour" (2000, p. 11)

Thus, according to the Baptist denomination, a person must repent of his or her sins, and must believe that Jesus is the Son of God before that person can be saved. This teaching of the Baptist doctrine is accurate, as far as it goes. The Bible does explicitly state that a person must repent (Luke 13:3-5; Acts 2:38) and believe in Christ (John 3:36; Romans 10:11). However, it is at this point that the Baptist denomination inconsistently insists that belief and repentance are **not** works, but that water baptism **is** a work.

Are baptism, faith, and repentance works? The Bible teaches that we are **not** saved by works (Titus 3:4-7; Ephesians 2:9). Yet the Bible clearly teaches we **are** saved by works (James 2:14-24). Since inspiration guarantees that the Scriptures will never contradict themselves, it is obvious that **two different kinds of works** are under consideration in these passages.

The New Testament mentions at least three kinds of works: (1) works of the Law of Moses (Galatians 2:16; Romans 3:20); (2) works of the flesh (Galatians 5:19-21); and (3) works resulting from obedience of faith (James 2:14-24). This last category is often referred to as "works of God." This phrase does not mean works **performed by** God, but works **approved by** God (Thayer, 1958, p. 248). Consider the following example from Jesus' statements in John 6:27-29:

> "Do not labor for the food which perishes, but for the food which endures to everlasting life, which the Son of Man will give you, because God the Father has set His seal on Him." Then they said to Him, "What shall **we do**, that **we may work** the works of God?" Jesus answered and said to them, "This is the work of God, that you believe in Him whom He sent" (emp. added).

Within this context, Christ made it clear that there are works that humans must **do** to receive eternal life. Moreover, the passage affirms that believing itself is a work ("This is the **work** of God, that you **believe** in Him whom He sent"). It therefore follows that if one is saved **without any type of works**, then he is saved **without belief**, because **belief is a work**. Such a conclusion would throw the Bible into hopeless confusion!

But what about baptism? The New Testament specifically excludes baptism from the class of human meritorious works unrelated to redemption. The context of Titus 3:4-7 reveals the following information: (1) We **are not saved** by works of righteousness that we do by ourselves. (2) We **are saved** by the "washing of regeneration" (i.e., baptism), exactly as 1 Peter 3:21 states; (3) Thus, baptism is excluded from all works of human righteousness that men contrive, but is itself a "work of God" (i.e., required and approved by God) necessary for salvation. When one is raised from the watery grave of baptism, it is according to the "working of God" (Colossians 2:12), and not any manmade plan. No one can maintain (justifiably) that baptism is a meritorious work of human design. When we are baptized, we are completely passive. Baptism is something that is done **to** a person, not **by** a person. Saving faith consists of the "works of God," which are belief, repentance, confession, and baptism—all commanded by the Scriptures for one who would receive salvation as the gift of God (Romans 6:23).

It is also interesting to note that the two books in which the apostle Paul condemns salvation by works of the Law the most vehemently (Romans and Galatians) are the very two books that relate the fact that water baptism puts a person into Christ (Romans 6:3; Galatians 3:27).

What about Paul's Statement, "Christ Sent Me not to Baptize"?

If it is the case that baptism is essential for salvation, why did the apostle John write: "Therefore, when the Lord knew that the Pharisees had heard that Jesus made and baptized more disciples than John (**though Jesus Himself did not baptize**, but His disciples), He left Judea and departed again to Galilee" (John 4:1-3, emp. added)? And why did the apostle Paul write to the church at Corinth: "**I thank God that I baptized none of you** except Crispus and Gaius, lest anyone should say that I had baptized in my own name... **For Christ did not send me to baptize, but to preach the gospel**" (1 Corinthians 1:14-17, emp. added)? Do these statements indicate that baptism is **not** necessary for a person to be saved? No, they do not.

First, John did not indicate that Jesus thought baptism was unnecessary. He merely stated the fact that Jesus did not personally—physically—do the baptizing; rather, His disciples did (John 4:2). The phrase in 4:1 regarding Jesus "baptizing" more disciples than John is simply a figure of speech where a person is represented as doing something when, in fact, he merely supplies the means for doing it. For example, Joseph indicated on one occasion that his brothers sold him into Egypt (Genesis 45:4-5; cf. Acts 7:9), when actually they sold him to the Ishmaelites (who then sold him into Egypt).

This is a well-known principle in law—a person who acts through another to break the law (e.g., paying someone to commit murder) is deemed by authorities to be guilty of breaking the law himself. Similarly, Jesus did not **personally** baptize anyone. But, **His teaching and influence** caused it to be done. Jesus, the subject, is mentioned, but it is the circumstance of His influence that is intended. His teaching was responsible for people being baptized. Thus, this passage actually implies that Jesus commanded that His listeners be baptized, and in no way contradicts teachings found elsewhere in the Bible.

Second, Paul's statements in his letter to the church at Corinth must be taken in their proper context in order to understand their true meaning. In 1 Corinthians 1:10-17, Paul was dealing with the division that was plaguing the Corinthian Christians. He had heard of the controversy in Corinth, and begged them to stand united, and to resolve their differences.

> Now I plead with you, brethren, by the name of our Lord Jesus Christ, that you all speak the same thing, and that there be no divisions among you, but that you be perfectly joined together in the same mind and in the same judgment. For it has been declared to me concerning you, my brethren, by those of Chloe's household, that there are contentions among you. Now I say this, that each of you says, "I am of Paul," or "I am of Apollos," or "I am of Cephas," or "I am of Christ." Is Christ divided? Was Paul crucified for you? Or were you baptized in the name of Paul?

> I thank God that I baptized none of you except Crispus and Gaius, lest anyone should say that I had baptized in my own name. Yes, I also baptized the household of Stephanas. Besides, I do not know whether I baptized any other. For Christ did not send me to baptize, but to preach the gospel, not with wisdom of words, lest the cross of Christ should be made of no effect (1 Corinthians 1:10-17).

Later, Paul added:

> For where there are envy, strife, and divisions among you, are you not carnal and behaving like mere men? For when one says, "I am of Paul," and another, "I am of Apollos," are you not carnal? Who then is Paul, and who is Apollos, but ministers through whom you believed, as the Lord gave to each one? I planted, Apollos watered, but God gave the increase. So then neither he who plants is anything, nor he who waters, but God who gives the increase (1 Corinthians 3:3-7).

When a person reads 1 Corinthians 1:14-17 in view of the problem of division in Corinth that Paul was addressing in chapter one and throughout this letter, he or she has a better understanding of Paul's statements regarding baptism. He was **not** indicating that baptism was unnecessary, but that people should not glory in the one who baptizes them. Some of the Corinthians were putting more emphasis on **who** baptized them, than on the **one body of Christ to which a person is added when he or she is baptized** (cf. Acts 2:41,47; Ephesians 4:4).

Paul was thankful that he did not personally baptize any more Corinthians than he did, lest they boast in **his** name, rather than in the name of **Christ** (1:15). Likely, this is the same reason why "Jesus Himself did not baptize, but His disciples." Imagine the spiritual snobbery that some immature Christians might have exhibited if the Messiah had baptized them personally (not to mention the fact that if Jesus were doing the baptizing, then it would most likely have consumed His entire day, because those being immersed would most likely have wanted the Savior to do it instead of one of the apostles). Along these lines, Paul understood that the fewer people he personally baptized, the less likely they were to rejoice in his name.

It is ironic that 1 Corinthians 1:13 has been used to argue against the necessity of baptism for salvation, when Paul implied that the only way to be saved is to be baptized into the name of Christ, saying, "Was Paul crucified for you? Or were you baptized in the name of Paul?" Paul wanted converts to tie themselves to the Savior, not to himself. He knew that "there is salvation in no one else" but Jesus, "for there is no other name under heaven that has been given among men, by which we must be saved" (Acts 4:12). Paul concerned himself with preaching, and, like Jesus, left others to do the baptizing.

When Paul stated, "Christ did not send me to baptize, but to preach the gospel," he meant that preaching was his main work, and that others could immerse the converts. He did not mean by this statement that **baptism** is unimportant, but that the **baptizer** is inconsequential.

Is Salvation the Result of "Baptismal Regeneration"?

Is the forgiveness of sins that results from being baptized due to some special power within the water? No. "Baptismal regeneration" is the false idea that there is a miraculous power in the water that produces salvation (i.e., regeneration). An examination of the Old Testament (which contains things "for our learning" [Romans 15:4]) provides important instruction regarding this principle. When Naaman the leper was told by Elisha to dip seven times in the Jordan River, at first he refused, but eventually obeyed—and was healed. However, there was no meritorious power in the muddy waters of the Jordan. Naaman was healed because He did exactly what God commanded him to do, in exactly the way God commanded him to do it.

The New Testament presents the same principle. Jesus once encountered a man born blind (John 9). Then the Lord spat on the ground, made a spittle/clay mixture, and placed it on the man's eyes. He then instructed the man to "go, wash in the pool of Siloam" (John 9:7). Was there medicinal power in Siloam's waters? No. It was the man's obedient faith that produced the end result, not some miraculous power in the water.

What would have happened if the man had refused to obey Christ, or had altered the Lord's command? Suppose the man had reasoned: "If I wash in Siloam, some may think I am trusting in the **water** to be healed. Others may think that I am attempting to perform some kind of 'work' to 'merit' regaining my sight. Therefore I simply will 'have faith in' Christ, but I will **not** wash in the pool of Siloam." Would the man have been healed?

What if Noah, during the construction of the ark, had followed God's instructions to the letter, except that he decided to build the ark out of a material other than the gopher wood that God had commanded? Would Noah and his family have been saved? No. Noah would have been guilty of violating God's commandments, since he had not done **exactly** as God commanded him. Did not Jesus Himself say: "If you love me, **keep My commandments**" (John 14:15, emp. added)?

Peter used the case of Noah to discuss the relationship of baptism to salvation. He stated: "There is also an antitype which now saves us—baptism (not the removal of the filth of the flesh, but the answer of a good conscience toward God), through the resurrection of Jesus Christ" (1 Peter 3:21). Just as Noah and his family were transported from a polluted environment of corruption into a realm of deliverance, so in baptism we are moved from the polluted environment of defilement into a realm of redemption. Notice that Peter insisted that the physical waters of baptism do not remove the dirt from the body. Instead, the obedience to God's command puts a person in contact with the blood of Jesus, which in turn removes the sin from the soul. The power of baptism to remove sin lies not in the water, but in the God Who commanded the sinner to be baptized in the first place.

What About the Thief on the Cross?

Many people dismiss water baptism as a prerequisite to salvation on the grounds that "the thief on the cross was not baptized." The thought is that since the thief was suspended on the cross when Jesus said to him, "Today you will be with Me in paradise" (Luke 23:43), he was being pronounced saved by Christ without being required to be baptized. As one well-known preacher put it, "There was no water within 10 miles of the cross." Please give consideration to two important observations.

First, the thief may well have been baptized **prior** to being placed on the cross. Consider the scriptural evidence that points to this conclusion as at least a viable possibility. Matthew 3:5-6 says, "Then Jerusalem, all Judea, and all the region around the Jordan" when out to John the Baptizer and were baptized, and John 4:1-2 states that Jesus and His disciples baptized more people than John (see also Mark 1:4-5; Luke 3:21; 7:29-30). If the thief had already submitted to baptism, there would have been no need for him to be re-baptized. He simply would have needed to repent of his post-baptism thievery and acknowledge his sins—which the text plainly indicates that he did.

Baptism

Second, and most important, the real issue pertains to an extremely crucial feature of Bible interpretation. This feature of understanding the Bible is so critical that, if a person does not grasp it, his effort to sort out Bible teaching, in order to arrive at correct conclusions, will be hopeless. This principle was spotlighted by Paul when he wrote to Timothy and told him he must "rightly divide the word of truth" (2 Timothy 2:15). In other words, if one simply takes the entire Bible—all 66 books—and treats them as if everything that is said applies directly and equally to everyone, his effort to be in harmony with God's Word will be hopeless and futile.

For example, if a person turned to Genesis 6 and read where God instructed Noah to build a boat, if he did not study enough to determine whether such instruction applied to himself, he would end up building his **own** boat—the entire time thinking that God wanted him to do so. The Bible is literally filled with commands, instructions, and requirements that were **not intended to be duplicated** by people living today. Does God forbid you and me from eating a certain fruit (Genesis 2:17; 3:3)? Does God want you and me to offer our son as a burnt offering (Genesis 22:2)? Are we commanded to load up our possessions and leave our homeland (Genesis 12:1)? Moving to the New Testament, does God want you to sell everything you have and give it to the poor (Matthew 19:21)? Does God expect you to leave everything, quit your job, and devote yourself full time to spiritual pursuits (Matthew 4:20; 19:27; Mark 10:28; Luke 5:28)? The point is that the entire Bible applies to the entire human race. However, careful and diligent study is necessary to determine **how** it applies. We must understand the biblical distinction between the application of the **principles** of the Bible and the **specific details**.

Here, then, is the central point as it pertains to the relevance of the thief on the cross: Beginning at Creation, all humans were responsible for obeying the laws of God that were given to them at that time. Bible students typically call this period of time the Patriarchal Dispensation. During this period, which lasted from Creation to roughly the time of the cross, non-Jews were subject to a body of legislation passed down by God through the fathers of family clans. In approximately 1,500 B.C., God removed the descendants of Abraham from Egyptian bondage, took them out into the Sinai desert, and gave them their own law code (the Law of Moses). Jews were subject to that body of legal information from that time until it, too, was terminated at the cross of Christ. The following passages substantiate these statements: Matthew 27:51; Romans 2:12-16; Galatians 3:7-29; Ephesians 2:11-22; Colossians 2:11-17. The book of Hebrews addresses this subject extensively.

To get to the heart of the matter quickly, read especially Hebrews 9:15-17. When one "correctly handles the Word of truth," one sees that the Bible teaches that when Christ died on the cross, Mosaic Law came to an end

At that point, all humans on the planet were called to obey **the law of Christ** (Galatians 6:2). The law of Christ consists strictly of information that is intended to be in effect **after** the death of Christ. It includes **some** of the things that Jesus and His disciples taught while He was still on Earth. But as regards the **specifics** of salvation, one must go to the rest of the New Testament (especially the book of Acts) in order to determine what one must do today to be saved. Beginning in Acts 2, the new covenant of Christ took effect, and every single individual who responded correctly to the preaching of the Gospel was **baptized in water in order to be forgiven of sin by the blood of Christ.** Every detail of an individual's conversion is not always mentioned, but a perusal of the book of Acts demonstrates decisively that water immersion was a **prerequisite** to forgiveness, along with faith, repentance, and confession of the deity of Christ (Acts 2:38,41; 8:12,13,16,36-38; 9:18; 10:47-48; 16:15,33; 18:8; 19:5; 22:16).

The thief was not subject to the New Testament command to be baptized into Christ's death (Romans 6:3-4), just as Moses, Abraham, and David were not subject to it. They all lived **prior** to the cross under different law codes. They could not have been baptized into Christ's death—**because He had not yet died!** In truth, the New Testament contains at least two other incidents in which Jesus forgave the sins of different individuals simply by pronouncing those sins forgiven. Matthew 9:1-8 and Mark

2:1-12 give parallel accounts of the story about the paralytic man who was lowered through the roof by his friends in the hope that Jesus would heal him. Upon seeing their faith, Jesus said, "Son, your sins are forgiven you" (Mark 2:5). Many in the crowd questioned Jesus' action, thinking that only God can forgive sins. And Jesus, to show that He was God in the flesh, healed the man to prove to the crowd that He had "power on earth to forgive sins" (Mark 2:10). A similar story is found in Luke 7:48, in which Jesus forgave the sins of a sinful woman who washed His feet. There is no doubt that while Jesus was alive on this Earth, He had the power to forgive sins. However, the establishment of His church and the launching of the Christian religion did not occur until **after** Christ's death, on the day of Pentecost around A.D. 30 in the city of Jerusalem (Acts 2). An honest and accurate appraisal of the biblical data forces us to conclude that the thief on the cross, and other New Testament incidents of immediate forgiveness accomplished directly by Christ while He was alive, are not appropriate examples of how people are to be saved this side of the cross.

Don't Some Baptist Churches Teach that Baptism is Essential for Salvation?

After being confronted with the biblical information concerning the necessity of baptism for the forgiveness of sins, some Baptists claim that their particular congregation **does** teach that baptism is essential for salvation.

A look at a telling statement made by a prominent Baptist writer throws serious doubt on this position. James Sullivan, in his book, *Baptist Polity: As I See It*, wrote: "In the 1830s, Alexander Campbell insisted that baptism be considered essential to salvation, **a purely rightist position in the theological world. Southern Baptists have never believed such**" (1998, p. 133). If a person believes that he was baptized for the remission of his sins in a Baptist church, I would challenge that person to call the preacher who baptized him and ask that preacher if he has ever baptized anyone for the remission of his sins in order to be saved. Such a call will quickly reveal that most every Baptist preacher (or church) views baptism as unnecessary for salvation and (according to the denomination) in no way connected to the forgiveness of sins.

When Should a Person be Re-baptized?

As we have seen, the word "baptism" means immersion. When a person is baptized, he or she is completely covered or buried with water. This is the proper, New Testament **action** of baptism. But the truth of the matter is, sometimes a person can get the **method** of baptism right and still not be properly baptized in accordance with God's will. For instance, suppose that a person had been paid $100 if he agrees to be immersed in water by a minister? Is that person's baptism valid according to Scripture? Or suppose that a person is baptized in the name of Paul?

Is his baptism New Testament baptism? In truth, there are many reasons to be baptized that would invalidate a person's baptism in God's sight.

In Acts 19, the Bible gives a brief story of several men who had been immersed in water, yet they were instructed to be baptized again (Acts 19:1-7).

> And it happened, while Apollos was at Corinth, that Paul, having passed through the upper regions, came to Ephesus. And finding some disciples he said to them, "Did you receive the Holy Spirit when you believed?" So they said to him, "We have not so much as heard whether there is a Holy Spirit." And he said to them, "Into what then were you baptized?" So they said, "Into John's baptism." Then Paul said, "John indeed baptized with a baptism of repentance, saying to the people that they should believe on Him who would come after him, that is, on Christ Jesus." When they heard this, they were baptized in the name of the Lord Jesus. And when Paul had laid hands on them, the Holy Spirit came upon them, and they spoke with tongues and prophesied. Now the men were about twelve in all.

What about these men who were re-baptized? The question must surely be raised: **why** were they re-baptized? Before offering an answer to this question, let us note some things of importance relating to John's baptism, which was the baptism they had received. First, John's baptism was to please ("in order to obey") God, since it was commanded by God during the life of John.

Second, it was for those who "should believe on Him who would come" (Acts 19:4) and, therefore, for people who accepted the deity of Christ. Third, it was for remission of sins (Mark 1:4). Now, with these three points in mind, **why** were the men in Acts 19 re-baptized? It will not do to merely say, "John's baptism was no longer valid." The obvious question is, **why** wasn't it? It was immersion. And it was for forgiveness of sins. The point I am trying to get across is this: these men were re-baptized because they **did not know enough!** And they **could have been baptized with a valid baptism, had they known enough.**

We see that a person must **know** that he is being baptized by the authority of the Father, the Son (Jesus Christ), and the Holy Spirit (Matthew 28:19-20). Peter, inspired by the Holy Spirit, boldly stated concerning the name of Jesus Christ that "there is no other name under heaven given among men by which we must be saved" (Acts 4:12). A person might be baptized in the name of Martin Luther, Muhammad, or Mahatma Gandhi, but only baptism **by the authority of Christ** will be able to save a person eternally.

Another essential fact that a person must **know** in order for his baptism to be valid is the fact that he was lost before he was baptized. When we look at the book of Acts and the epistles, we find that people who were baptized properly understood that they were unsaved before baptism. Peter instructed his listeners to be baptized "for the forgiveness" of their sins (Acts 2:38). Ananias told Saul to "arise and be baptized, and wash away your sins, calling on the name of the Lord" (Acts 22:16). Paul told those who eventually composed the church in Rome that they had been baptized "into Christ Jesus" (Romans 6:3), and he told the Ephesian church that any person who was not in Christ had no hope and was without God (Ephesians 2:12). In baptism, the alien sinner recognizes that he or she dies to sin, and rises from the water to walk "in newness of life" (Romans 6:4). [A person who believes that he was saved **before** baptism must contend that he was already walking in "newness of life" before being immersed.] Various other terminology is used to describe water baptism in the New Testament (1 Peter 3:21; Galatians 3:27; Acts 8:38), yet in every case, this terminology shows that baptism is the dividing line between the lost and the saved. According to the New Testament examples and explanations of baptism, every person who was acceptably baptized with the proper understanding knew that he or she was still in sin before his or her water baptism.

A study of New Testament baptism shows that, not only must a person be baptized by complete immersion "to obey God" by the authority of the Father, Son, and Holy Spirit, but that person also must understand that he or she is lost before his water baptism. Any person who did not understand this at the time of baptism should be re-baptized with this understanding in accordance with the divine pattern set for us in Acts 19:1-7.

How Important is the Doctrine of Baptism?

If a person or group of people teaches that salvation can be obtained in any other way than the Bible teaches, then that person or group of people falls directly under the curse of God. Paul, in Galatians 1:8-9, put it this way: "But even if we, or an angel from heaven, preach any other gospel to you than what we have preached to you, let him be accursed. As we have said before, so now I say again, if anyone preaches any other gospel to you than what you have received, let him be accursed."

Following Paul's reasoning, if the Baptist church teaches that a person **can** be saved without contacting Christ's blood in water baptism, but the Bible teaches that a person **cannot** be saved without contacting Christ's blood in water baptism, then the Baptist church is under the curse of God. Of course, this sounds terribly harsh to say about a denomination that seems to be following the Bible so closely. And, there are many fine people in the Baptist denomination who are kind, generous, and highly moral. But there are many highly moral pagans as well. And many kind, generous Hindus and Muslims live in our world today. Yet, the truths in these various religions cannot compensate for their false teachings, and the moral nature of their adherents does not change the fact that the religions are wrong according to God and His Word.

Chapter 3

THE PERSEVERANCE OF THE SAINTS

Another widely taught doctrine of the Baptist denomination is known as "the perseverance of the saints." This doctrine basically states that once a person is saved, then that person cannot fall from his or her saved position. "This concept is sometimes called 'the security of the believer' or 'once saved, always saved'" (Hobbs, 1964, p. 103). The *Baptist Faith and Message,* under Article V, states:

> All true believers endure to the end. Those whom God has accepted in Christ, and sanctified by His Spirit, will never fall away from the state of grace, but shall persevere to the end. Believers may fall into sin through neglect and temptation, whereby they grieve the Spirit, impair their graces and comforts, and bring reproach on the cause of Christ and temporal judgments on themselves; yet they shall be kept by the power of God through faith unto salvation (2000, p. 12).

Herschel Hobbs, in *What Baptists Believe*, wrote: "Redemption in the beginning depends upon what God does, not man. Its permanence likewise depends upon what God has done and continues to do, not man" (1964, p. 104). From Hobbs' statement, one can see that the gist of this doctrine says that, once a person has been saved, nothing that person does after his or her salvation can cause the loss of that salvation. Hobbs clearly stated that the Baptist denomination teaches that once a person is saved, there is "no possibility of losing such a relationship" (p. 90). In his book, *Foundations of the Faith: The Doctrines Baptists Believe,* Roy Edgemon wrote:

> When a person truly accepts Christ as Savior, he receives a guarantee that he will not again be lost (see John 3:16; 10:27-29; Phil. 1:5-6; 1 Peter 1:5). The truth of eternal security is a great comfort. Our salvation is not dependent on our own strength, but on God's. If it were dependent on us, most of us would be lost in the end (1999, p. 77).

This doctrine, coming from John Calvin, has permeated the Baptist denomination for hundreds of years. In the Philadelphia Confession of Faith of 1742, the crafters of that particular Baptist confession wrote:

> Those whom God hath accepted in the Beloved, effectually called and sanctified by His Spirit, and given the precious faith of His elect unto, can neither totally nor finally fall from the state of grace....

> This perseverance of the saints depends not upon their own free will, but upon the immutability of the decree of election (George and George, 1999, p. 75).

As comforting as this doctrine may appear—that a person cannot lose his or her salvation—it is another Baptist doctrine that stands in direct opposition to the text of the New Testament. The following pages list but a few of the New Testament passages which prove that a person can be in a saved state but, due to unfaithfulness and disobedience, may fall away from God's grace and end up in a lost condition.

Numerous statements made by Jesus Christ Himself militate against the idea that "once a person is saved, then he is always saved." After Jesus told the parable of the sower, His disciples asked for further clarification as to the meaning of the parable. Answering their request, Jesus declared:

> Now the parable is this: The seed is the word of God. Those by the wayside are the ones who hear; then the devil comes and takes away the word out of their hearts, lest they should believe and be saved. But the ones on the rock are those who, when they hear, receive the word with joy; and these have no root, who believe for a while and in time of temptation fall away. Now the ones that fell among thorns are those who, when they have heard, go out and are choked with cares, riches, and pleasures of life, and bring no fruit to maturity. But the ones that fell

on the good ground are those who, having heard
the word with a noble and good heart, keep it and
bear fruit with patience (Luke 8:11-15).

From this explanation, it is clear that some people "receive the word with joy" and "believe for a while." Jesus pictured some individuals who are fully saved and in a state of grace, but when temptation arises, they "fall away." The question must be asked, "From what do they fall away?" They fall away from the saved state of grace that they had once occupied, because they are not like those represented by the good ground, who hear the Word and "keep it and bear fruit with patience." Failure to continue in the Word, according to Jesus, will cause one to "fall away."

On another occasion, Jesus used a vine to illustrate this same principle. In John 15, He proclaimed:

> I am the true vine, and My Father is the vinedresser. Every branch in Me that does not bear fruit **He takes away**; and every branch that bears fruit He prunes, that it may bear more fruit. You are already clean because of the word which I have spoken to you. Abide in Me, and I in you. As the branch cannot bear fruit of itself, unless it abides in the vine, neither can you, unless you abide in Me. I am the vine, you are the branches. He who abides in Me, and I in him, bears much fruit; for without Me you can do nothing. **If anyone does not abide in Me**, he is cast out as a branch and is withered; and they gather them and throw them into the fire, and they are burned (John 15:1-6, emp. added).

The Perseverance of the Saints

From the text, one can read that abiding in Christ is the only way to inherit salvation and avoid being thrown "into the fire." Jesus presented the situation in which some branches at one time were "in" Him, but, due to their barrenness, the Father "takes away" those branches. In the conclusion of the passage, Jesus described a person who does not abide in Him, and thus is "cast out as a branch and is withered." Before this individual was cast out, he was obviously abiding and growing in the vine, else, why would he "wither" upon being cast out?

Other narratives can be cited in which Jesus taught that a person can fall from grace. To illustrate the nature of God's forgiveness, Jesus told the following parable.

> Therefore the kingdom of heaven is like a certain king who wanted to settle accounts with his servants. And when he had begun to settle accounts, one was brought to him who owed him ten thousand talents. But as he was not able to pay, his master commanded that he be sold, with his wife and children and all that he had, and that payment be made. The servant therefore fell down before him, saying, "Master, have patience with me, and I will pay you all." **Then the master of that servant was moved with compassion, released him, and forgave him the debt**. But that servant went out and found one of his fellow servants who owed him a hundred denarii; and he laid hands on him and took him by the throat, saying, "Pay me what you owe!" So his fellow servant fell down at his feet

and begged him, saying, "Have patience with me, and I will pay you all." And he would not, but went and threw him into prison till he should pay the debt. So when his fellow servants saw what had been done, they were very grieved, and came and told their master all that had been done. Then his master, after he had called him, said to him, "You wicked servant! I forgave you all that debt because you begged me. Should you not also have had compassion on your fellow servant, just as I had pity on you?" **And his master was angry, and delivered him to the torturers until he should pay all that was due to him.** So My heavenly Father also will do to you if each of you, from his heart, does not forgive his brother his trespasses (Matthew 18:23-35, emp. added).

In this passage, Jesus described a man whom the master "forgave" of a great debt. After forgiveness was granted, however, the wicked servant went and found his fellow servant who owed him a small amount of money. Refusing to forgive his fellow servant, the wicked servant was reported to the master. Upon hearing of the wicked servant's unforgiving attitude, the master reinstated the debt that had previously been forgiven. This parable shows the conditional nature of God's forgiveness toward us today. It also proves that even if a person's sins have been forgiven in the past, unless that person continues to behave in a way pleasing to the Master, he will be lost.

The Perseverance of the Saints 49

The statements of Jesus recorded in the book of Revelation written to the seven churches of Asia offer even more testimony that militates against the "perseverance of the saints." In His comments to the church at Ephesus, He told them that they had left their first love. In His reprimand of the church, He instructed the brethren to "repent and do the first works, or else I will come to you quickly and remove your lampstand from its place—unless you repent" (Revelation 2:5).

Along a similar line of reasoning, Jesus informed the church at Pergamos that false teachers had infiltrated their congregation, and were teaching destructive doctrines. Jesus then told the church: "Repent, or else I will come to you quickly and will fight against them with the sword of my mouth" (Revelation 2:16). To the church at Sardis, He wrote that they had a name that they were alive, but they were really dead. He further noted that He had not found their works perfect before God. In keeping with His statements to the other sinning churches, He said: "Remember therefore how you have received and heard: hold fast and repent. Therefore if you will not watch, I will come upon you as a thief, and you will not know what hour I will come upon you" (3:3). To the lukewarm church of the Laodiceans, Jesus wrote that He would "spew" them out of His mouth due to their lackluster profession of faith (3:16).

Jesus' statements to the sinful churches in Asia show that the salvation of church members was conditioned upon their continued faithfulness to His commands. In

Revelation 2:10, Jesus told the church at Smyrna: "Be faithful until death, and I will give you the crown of life." He implied, by this statement, that all those who would not remain faithful until death would not receive the crown of life.

The apostle Paul also spoke out on numerous occasions against the "once saved, always saved" idea. He wrote to Timothy:

> Now the Spirit expressly says that in latter times some will **depart from the faith**, giving heed to deceiving spirits and doctrines of demons, speaking lies in hypocrisy, having their own conscience seared with a hot iron… Take heed to yourself and to the doctrine. **Continue in them**, for in doing this you will save both yourself and those who hear you (1 Timothy 4:1,2,16, emp. added).

These verses indicate that certain individuals would **depart** from the faith. In order to depart, however, one must have at one time been **in** the faith. Also, Timothy's salvation was conditioned upon his continuance in the doctrines of the apostles. If Timothy continued in those doctrines, then he would "save" both himself and his hearers. But if he did not continue in those doctrines, then he would be lost.

To the Corinthians, Paul wrote: "Moreover, brethren, I declare to you the gospel which I preached to you, which also you received and in which you stand, by which also you are saved, **if** you hold fast that word which I preached to you—unless you believed in vain" (1 Corinthians 15:1-2, emp. added). Here again, the inspired Paul warned the Corinthians that their salvation would be assured **if** they held fast God's Word. The direct implication from this verse is that if they did **not** hold fast to that word, then they would not be saved.

One of the most crushing blows to the "once saved, always saved" doctrine is found in Paul's letter to the Galatians. To the Galatians, Paul vehemently attempted to persuade the Christians in that city not to return to the old Law of Moses. Since salvation comes only through Christ, he argued, then the old Law cannot save a person. What would happen to those Christians who attempted to go back to the old Law, trusting it for salvation? Paul wrote:

> Stand fast therefore in the liberty by which Christ has made us free, and do not be entangled again with a yoke of bondage. Indeed I, Paul, say to you that if you become circumcised, Christ will profit you nothing. And I testify again to every man who becomes circumcised that he is a debtor to keep the whole law. **You have become estranged from Christ, you who attempt to be justified by law; you have fallen from grace** (Galatians 5:1-4, emp. added).

Those who believe in the perseverance of the saints have a difficult time dealing with this passage, since it explicitly states that anyone who attempts to go back to the old Law has "fallen from grace." This statement from Paul's pen lies in direct contradiction to the statement made in the *Baptist Faith and Message*, that those once saved "will never fall away from the state of grace." Is it possible, today, for a person to return to his former religion or state of disobedience after his conversion to Christianity? Certainly. What will such an action cause? Such an action will cause those Christians to fall from grace and be lost—just as it caused Galatian Christians in Paul's day to be lost.

Paul understood the conditional nature of a Christian's salvation so well that he even indicated that his own salvation would be in jeopardy if he did not continue in the faith. In 1 Corinthians 9:27, he asserted: "But I discipline my body and bring it into subjection, lest, when I have preached to others, I myself should become disqualified."

The inspired apostle John also wrote concerning the conditional nature of salvation. In 1 John 2:24-25, we read: "Therefore let that abide in you which you heard from the beginning. **If** what you heard from the beginning abides in you, you also will abide in the Son and in the Father. And this is the promise that He has promised us—eternal life" (emp. added). John, in agreement with Jesus and Paul, conditioned the salvation of his readers upon their choice to abide in the doctrine that they had received.

Advocates of the "once saved, always saved" doctrine point to certain verses that they believe support their doctrine. When these verses are analyzed closely, however, it becomes evident that they do not support the doctrine, and thus do not contradict the various passages listed above.

One such verse is John 5:24, which has Jesus on record as stating, "Most assuredly, I say to you, he who hears My word and believes in Him who sent Me has everlasting life, and shall not come into judgment, but has passed from death into life." Many of those who accept the idea of the perseverance of the saints point to this verse and declare that the phrase "has everlasting life" proves the "once saved, always saved" idea. It should be noted, however, that having everlasting life is conditioned upon whether a person "hears" and "believes." Those two words are not one-time actions, but rather, describe a person who **continues** to hear and **continues** to believe. (These two words in Greek are present participles that denote continuous action.) Thus, whoever continues to hear and believe Jesus has everlasting life.

Another important aspect of this verse that sometimes goes unnoticed is the fact that the biblical usage of the word "believe" often implies obedience that accompanies that belief. In 1 Peter 2:7, the apostle wrote: "Therefore, to you who **believe**, He is precious; but to those who are **disobedient**, 'The stone which the builders rejected Has become the chief cornerstone'" (emp.

added). In this verse, Peter regarded disobedience as the opposite of belief. The Hebrew writer also equated unbelief and disobedience. In Hebrews 3:18-19, the Israelites were not allowed into the Promised Land because they "did not obey" (3:18). But the next verse states, "So we see that they could not enter in because of unbelief" (3:19). And Hebrews 4:6 also declares that they "did not enter because of disobedience."

Indeed, when a person diligently studies the New Testament, it should become clear that mere mental acceptance of the fact that Jesus is the Son of God has never been enough to save. The gospel of Mark records that Jesus went into a synagogue on the Sabbath and met a man with an unclean spirit. The unclean spirit cried out, "Let us alone! What have we to do with You, Jesus of Nazareth? Did You come to destroy us? I know who You are—the Holy One of God" (Mark 1:24). Truly, the unclean spirit believed that Jesus was the Christ, the Son of God. Yet that knowledge did not put the unclean spirit in a saved condition. In like manner, the gospel of John records that "even among the rulers many believed in Him [Jesus—KB], but because of the Pharisees they did not confess Him, lest they should be put out of the synagogue; for they loved the praise of men more than the praise of God" (John 12:42-43). Would anyone contend that these Jewish leaders should be saved based on their mental assent to Jesus' deity, even though they desired to please men instead of God? James wrote: "You believe that there is one God. You do well. Even the demons believe—and tremble! But do you want to know, O foolish man, that faith without works is dead?" (James 2:19-20). Saving faith in the New Testament always entails the mental acceptance that Jesus is the Christ, the Son of God, **combined with obedience to His commands**.

Another passage used to support the "perseverance of the saints" can be found in Romans 8:38-39, where Paul wrote: "For I am persuaded that neither death, nor life, nor angels nor principalities nor powers, nor things present nor things to come nor height nor depth, nor any other created thing, shall be able to separate us from the love of God which is in Christ Jesus our Lord." Does this passage teach that a person cannot be separated from Christ? If we look closely, we see that the passage teaches that **no outside force** such as death or the devil can separate a faithful believer from his God. However, this verse does not say that a person cannot separate himself from the love of God. In fact, when we look at the beginning of Romans 8, we see that this salvation is conditioned upon living "in the spirit." Paul wrote: "Therefore, brethren, we are debtors—not to the flesh, to live according to the flesh. For **if** you live according to the flesh you will die; but **if** by the spirit you put to death the deeds of the body, you will live" (emp. added). In this chapter, as in other passages discussing the salvation of the saints, a continued state of salvation is based upon the actions of those who are being saved. Paul declared that nothing could separate us from the love of Christ—**if** we walk by the Spirit. The obvious implication is that **if** we do not walk by the Spirit, then we separate ourselves from the love of Christ.

Indeed, every verse used to "prove" the perseverance of the saints, when examined in its proper context, can be shown to be conditioned on the continued faithful behavior of the one being saved. The "once saved, always saved" doctrine held by the Baptist church does not square with the Bible's teaching on salvation. The Bible clearly states in numerous passages that certain people were, at one time saved, but due to their own unfaithfulness, lost that salvation. The teachings of the Baptist church offer a false sense of security to its adherents. Salvation can be lost, and that was one of the main reasons the books and epistles of Romans through Revelation were written. The recipients of these teachings were already Christians, but they needed further instruction, admonition, and encouragement so that they would be "faithful unto death."

In reality, even some Baptists in past generations recognized the truth of these statements. Thomas Helwys was the primary author of the 27 articles published in 1611 which, according to McBeth, "form one of the first Baptist confessions of faith and thus one of the earliest systematic expressions of Baptist theology" (1990, p. 39). Article 7 states:

> A righteous man may forsake his righteousness and perish (Ezekiel 18:24-26). And therefore let no man presume to think that because he hath, or had once grace, therefore he shall always have grace. **But let all men have assurance, that if they continue unto the end, they shall be saved. Let no man then presume**; but let all work out their salvation with fear and trembling (as quoted in McBeth, p. 40, emp. added, adapted from Old English).

It is truly sad that the Baptist denomination today has drifted far from Helwys' statement—and the New Testament's teaching—concerning the conditional nature of salvation. [For an exhaustive study of the doctrine of the perseverance of the saints, see *Life in the Son* by former Baptist preacher Robert Shank.]

Chapter 4

CHURCH ORGANIZATION

Another distinct doctrine of most forms of the Baptist denomination is the democratic nature of each autonomous congregation. Many things are put before the entire congregation or a board of deacons for them to cast their vote opposing or favoring. One of the things about which the congregations or deacons vote is whether or not to receive a person into their fellowship. J. Newton Brown, in his book, *A Baptist Church Manual*, wrote concerning this practice under a section titled "Rules of Church Order," Article I, "Reception of Members," Section 6: "No person shall be received as a member of this church if five members object to his or her admission" (1994, p. 34). Edward T. Hiscox, in his monumental work, *The Standard Manual for Baptist Churches*, wrote concerning those seeking fellowship in any Baptist congregation: "And while they cannot become members without baptism, yet it is the vote of the body which admits them to its fellowship on receiving baptism (1903, p. 22). The *Baptist Faith and Message* reads: "Each congregation operates under the Lordship of Christ through democratic processes" (p. 13, Article 6). Stan Norman wrote: "Baptist churches practice what some call 'pure democracy.' All the members of the church are equal citizens in Christ's kingdom, and the majority of the citizenry discerns the direction of God for the church" (2001b, p. 124).

This view, that each congregation is a democracy, jibes well with the western mindset that all people should have an equal voice in the decision-making process of a congregation. Democracy has worked well for those of us in the United States, and it is easy to see how such an idea has carried over into the Baptist denomination. This democratic view, however, does not harmonize with the biblical doctrine of church organization and operation.

In the New Testament, a group of elders, who met very strict qualifications, made the decisions for each congregation. Titus 1:5-9 and 1 Timothy 3:1-7 list the qualifications for these men. They are to be the spiritual overseers of each congregation. In Acts 20:17, Paul called to him the "elders (*presbuteros*) of the church" at Ephesus. In verse 28 of that same chapter, Paul told these elders to "take heed to yourselves and to all the flock, among which the Holy Spirit has made you overseers (*episkopos*), to shepherd (*poimaino*) the church of God...." In this same verse, Paul stated that these elders were the "overseers" (*episkopos*) and that they were "to shepherd" (*poimaino*). Paul's use of the phrase "to shepherd" is the source from which we get our word "pastor." The men given the spiritual oversight of each congregation are overseers or bishops (*episkopos*), and also are referred to as pastors (*poimen*—Ephesians 4:11) or elders (*presbuteros*). The Greek words used in the New Testament to describe these men and their functions are used interchangeably to describe the same office. Edward Hiscox wrote, "Titus is in like manner directed by Paul to place pastors over the churches in Crete. These **pastors** he calls **elders** in the fifth verse and **bishops** in the seventh. Here both terms are applied to the same persons, and must indicate the same office—Titus 1:5,7" (n.d., p. 91, emp. in orig.). Peter wrote that the elders were to shepherd (*poimaino*) the "flock of God serving as overseers" (*episkopos*), not as being "lords over those entrusted to you, but being examples to the flock" (1 Peter 5:1-4).

It is interesting to note, also, that the New Testament always presents a **plurality** of pastors for every congregation. We never read about a lone "pastor" or "bishop" ruling over a congregation or a group of congregations. Yet, in the Baptist denomination it is a common practice to appoint one pastor "over" a church. Brown, in *A Baptist Church Manual,* on several occasions, talks about "the pastor" of a congregation. And, in his discussion on conducting a business meeting, he says "the pastor of the church" should act as moderator (1994, p. 38). The New Testament never mentions or sanctions the "one pastor" system.

Furthermore, many of the "pastors" who are put over Baptist congregations do not meet the qualifications found in 1 Timothy 3 and Titus 1. Such qualifications as being the husband of one wife and having faithful children are not optional; they are required by God. It is interesting to note that the apostle Paul, who was probably not married (see 1 Corinthians 7:6-7), "did not refer to himself as a pastor" (Mosley, 1996, p. 67). But Peter, who we know was married (Matthew 8:14-15), did class himself with the bishops or pastors (1 Peter 5:1-4). Even if the New Testament allowed for one pastor to oversee an entire congregation (which it does not), that pastor still must meet the qualifications found in Paul's letters to Titus and Timothy.

In addition, the New Testament **never** presents the idea that the church is to be a "pure democracy." The elders are to make the spiritual decisions for the congregation (assuming, of course, that those decisions are in agreement with the "Chief Shepherd's" commandments as presented in 1 Peter 5:4). The various members of the congregation are to submit to the elders (1 Peter 5:5). Members of a congregation do not have the right to "vote" a person into or out of its fellowship. If a person has obeyed God's commands for salvation, he or she should be allowed into any congregation of the Lord's people, regardless of whether or not "five members object to his or her admission." Mosley, in *Basics for Baptists,* wrote: "The pastor and other church leaders may be helpful in developing church programs and policies, but all decisions should be approved by the gathered church" (1996, p. 66). His comment proves that the Baptist denomination does not have a group of pastors who make the spiritual decisions for each congregation. Rather, each Baptist congregation is ruled by "majority vote." Yet, the New Testament speaks in direct opposition to these teachings of Mosley and the Baptist denomination. Only with the true New Testament organization, where qualified, spiritually mature men make the decisions, can each congregation function properly under the ultimate headship of Christ (Ephesians 1:22-23).

Mosley admitted: "Baptists **have chosen** a form of church government that utilizes democratic processes under the lordship of Jesus Christ" (1996, p. 65, emp. added). But, if the Baptist denomination were the Lord's church, then it would not "choose" a form of church government that does not find its origin in the New Testament. Furthermore, the Lord's church has no right to "choose" which type of government it likes, dislikes, or thinks is more effective. The Lord's church is constrained to utilize the form of church government that its head, Christ, has chosen for it. Through the New Testament, we see that each congregation was to be under the oversight of a plurality of qualified elders. These men made the spiritual decisions for the congregation, and were not obliged to take their decisions before the congregation for a democratic vote.

Chapter 5

CONCLUSION

In Matthew 16:18, the Lord Jesus said that He would build His church, and the gates of Hades would not prevail against it. Paul, in his letter to the church at Ephesus, informed us that the church is the body of Christ (1:22-23), and that there is only one church that belongs to Jesus (4:4). The church of Jesus Christ is composed of those people who are following the teachings found in the New Testament. The church of the Lord must teach the same plan of salvation as the apostles taught in order to be the church. The one church that belongs to Christ must have the proper organization in order to be His church. The church of Christ must teach the correct doctrine of Jesus and the apostles as to the possibility of a person losing his or her salvation.

In Mark 4:13-20, Jesus told a parable about a sower who sowed seed on four different kinds of ground. The seed that was sown was the Word of God (4:14). When the Word of God falls on good and honest hearts, it produces Christians only and only Christians. Doctrines that produce something other than New Testament Christians are not products of the true Word of God.

The Baptist denomination is filled with many kind, sincere people who believe that they are members of the one true church that Jesus bought with His blood. When their basic doctrines are compared to the New Testament, however, the two stand in opposition to one another on several points. The Baptist denomination teaches that a person can be saved before water baptism; the New Testament teaches that a person must be immersed in water to be saved. The Baptist denomination teaches that a saved person cannot fall from his or her saved condition; the New Testament teaches that the saved can fall away. The Baptist denomination teaches that congregations of the church are "pure democracies" that often have only one pastor; the New Testament teaches that each congregation is overseen by a **plurality** of pastors who are responsible for the spiritual decisions of the church. The Baptist denomination, by the very fact that it is a **denomination**, teaches that dividing the church into differing denominations is acceptable; the New Testament insists that such divisions are wrong.

The Baptist denomination is a manmade religious organization that is not the Lord's church. The New Testament knows nothing of a Baptist Church or Baptist Christians. If you are a Baptist, I urge you, in a spirit of love, to

Conclusion

leave that denomination and begin your search for the Lord's church that is pictured in the New Testament. I urge you to be baptized into the death of Christ for the remission of your sins, just as the apostles in the New Testament taught (Acts 2:38). And I beseech you to rise from that water of baptism determined to be a Christian only and only a Christian.

Appendix A

"CALLING ON THE NAME OF THE LORD"

Many people within "Christendom" teach that an individual can be saved merely by professing a belief in Christ. While it is true that Peter and Paul declared, "Whoever calls on the name of the Lord shall be saved" (Acts 2:21; Romans 10:13; cf. Joel 2:32), it also is true that Jesus once stated: "Not everyone who says to Me, 'Lord, Lord,' shall enter the kingdom of heaven, but he who does the will of My Father in heaven" (Matthew 7:21; cf. Luke 6:46). Many professed Christians seem to equate "calling on the name of the Lord" with the idea of saying to Jesus, "Lord, save me." How can certain professed followers of Christ claim that they were saved by simply "calling out to Christ," when Christ Himself proclaimed that a mere calling upon Him will not save a person?

The key to correctly understanding the phrase "calling on the name of the Lord," is to recognize that more is involved in this action than a mere verbal petition directed toward God. The "call" mentioned in Acts 2:21, Romans 10:13, and Acts 22:16 (where Paul was "calling on the name of the Lord"), is not equated with the "call" ("Lord, Lord") of which Jesus spoke in the Sermon on the Mount (Matthew 7:21).

First, it is appropriate to mention that even in modern times, to "call on" someone frequently means more than simply making a request for something. When a doctor goes to the hospital to "call on" some of his patients, he does not merely walk into the room and say, "I just wanted to come by and say, 'Hello.' I wish you the best. Now pay me." On the contrary, he involves himself in a service. He examines the patient, listens to the patient's concerns, gives further instructions regarding the patient's anticipated recovery, and then oftentimes prescribes medication. All of these elements may be involved in a doctor "calling upon" a patient. In the mid-twentieth century, it was common for young men to "call on" young ladies. Again, this expression meant something different than just making a request.

Second, when an individual takes the time to study how the expression "calling on God" is used throughout Scripture, the only reasonable conclusion to draw is that, just as similar phrases sometimes have a deeper meaning in modern America, the expression "calling on God" often had a deeper meaning in Bible times. Take, for instance, Paul's statement recorded in Acts 25:11: "I appeal unto Caesar." The word "appeal" (*epikaloumai*) is the same word translated "call" (or "calling") in Acts 2:21,

22:16, and Romans 10:13. But Paul was not simply saying, "I'm calling on Caesar to save me." Paul's "calling" to Caesar involved his submission to him. It was not a mere verbal recognition of God, or a verbal petition to Him.

Those whom Paul (before his conversion to Christ) sought to bind in Damascus—**Christians** who were described as people "who call on Your [Jehovah's] name"—were not people who only prayed to God, but those who were serving the Lord, and who, by their obedience, were submitting themselves to His authority (cf. Matthew 28:18). Interestingly, Zephaniah 3:9 links one's "calling" with his "service": "For then I will restore to the peoples a pure language, **that they all may call on the name of the Lord, to serve Him with one accord**" (emp. added). When a person submits to the will of God, he can accurately be described as "calling on the Lord." Acts 2:21 and Romans 10:13 (among other passages) do not contradict Matthew 7:21, because to "call on the Lord" entails more than just pleading for salvation; it involves submitting to God's will. According to Colossians 3:17, every single act a Christian performs (in word or deed) should be carried out by Christ's authority. For a non-Christian receiving salvation, this is no different. In order to obtain salvation, a person must submit to the Lord's authority. This is what the passages in Acts 2:21 and Romans 10:13 are teaching; it is up to us to go elsewhere in the New Testament to learn **how** to call upon the name of the Lord.

After Peter quoted the prophecy of Joel, and told those in Jerusalem on Pentecost that "whoever calls on the name of the Lord shall be saved" (Acts 2:21), he told them **how** to go about "calling on the name of the Lord." The people in the audience in Acts 2 did not understand Peter's quotation of Joel to mean that an alien sinner must pray to God for salvation. [Their question in Acts 2:37 ("Men and brethren, what shall we do?") indicates such.] Furthermore, when Peter responded to their question, and told them what to do to be saved, he did not say, "I've already told you what to do. You can be saved by petitioning God for salvation through prayer. Just call on His name." On the contrary, Peter had to explain to them what it meant to "call on the name of the Lord." Instead of repeating this statement when the crowd sought further guidance from the apostles, Peter commanded them, saying, "Repent, and let every one of you be baptized in the name of Jesus Christ for the remission of sins" (2:38). Notice the parallel between Acts 2:21 and 2:38:

Acts 2:21	Whoever	Calls	On the name of the Lord	Shall be saved
Acts 2:38	Everyone of you	Repentance and baptism	In the name of Jesus Christ	For the remission of sins

Peter's non-Christian listeners learned that "calling on the name of the Lord for salvation" was equal to obeying the Gospel, which approximately 3,000 did that very day by repenting of their sins and being baptized into Christ (2:38,41).

But what about Romans 10:13? What is the "call" mentioned in this verse? Notice Romans 10:11-15:

> For the Scripture says, "Whoever believes on Him will not be put to shame." For there is no distinction between Jew and Greek, for the same Lord over all is rich to all who call upon Him. For **"whoever calls on the name of the Lord shall be saved." How then shall they call on Him in whom they have not believed?** And how shall they believe in Him of whom they have not heard? And how shall they hear without a preacher? And how shall they preach unless they are sent? As it is written: "How beautiful are the feet of those who preach the gospel of peace, who bring glad tidings of good things!" (emp. added).

Although this passage does not define precisely what is meant by one "calling on the name of the Lord," it does indicate that an alien sinner cannot "call" until after he has heard the Word of God and believed it. Such was meant by Paul's rhetorical questions: "How then shall they call on Him in whom they have not believed? And how shall they believe in Him of whom they have not heard?" Paul's statements in this passage are consistent with Peter's proclamations in Acts 2. It was only **after** the crowd on Pentecost believed in the resurrected Christ Whom Peter preached (as is evident by their being "cut to the heart," and their subsequent question, "Men and brethren, what shall we do?") that Peter told them how to call on the name of the Lord and be saved (2:38).

Perhaps the clearest description of what it means for an alien sinner to "call on the name of the Lord" is found in Acts 22. As the apostle Paul addressed the mob in Jerusalem, he spoke of his encounter with the Lord, Whom he asked, "What shall I do?" (22:10; cf. 9:6). The answer Jesus gave Him at that time was not "call on the name of the Lord." Instead, Jesus instructed him to "arise and go into Damascus, and there you will be told all things which are appointed for you to do" (22:10). Paul (or Saul—Acts 13:9) revealed his belief in Jesus as he went into the city and waited for further instructions. In Acts 9, we learn that during the next three days, while waiting to meet with Ananias, Paul fasted and prayed (vss. 9,11). Although some today might consider what Paul was doing at this point as "calling on the name of the Lord," Ananias, God's chosen messenger to Paul, did not think so. He did not tell Paul, "I see you have already called on God. Your sins are forgiven." After three days of fasting and praying, Paul was still **lost in his sins**. Even though he obviously **believed** at this point, and had prayed to God, he had yet to "call on the name of the Lord" for salvation.

When Ananias finally came to Paul, he told him: "Arise and be baptized, and wash away your sins, calling on the name of the Lord" (22:16). Ananias knew that Paul had not yet "called on the name of the Lord," just as Peter knew that those on Pentecost had not done so before his command to "repent and be baptized." Thus, Ananias instructed Paul to "be baptized, and wash away your sins." The participle phrase, "calling on the name of the Lord," describes what Paul was doing when he was baptized for the remission of his sins. Every non-Christian who desires to "call on the name of the Lord" to be saved, does so, not simply by crying out, "Lord, Lord" (cf. Matthew 7:21), or just by wording a prayer to God (e.g., Paul—Acts 9; 22; cf. Romans 10:13-14), but by obeying God's instructions to "repent and be baptized...in the name of Jesus Christ for the remission of your sins" (Acts 2:38).

This is not to say that repentance and baptism have always been (or are always today) synonymous with "calling on the name of the Lord." Abraham was not baptized when he "called upon the name of the Lord" (Genesis 12:8; cf. 4:26), because baptism was not demanded of God before New Testament times. And, as mentioned earlier, when the New Testament describes people who are already Christians as "calling on the name of the Lord" (Acts 9:14,21; 1 Corinthians 1:2), it certainly does not mean that Christians continually were being baptized for the remission of their sins after having been baptized to become Christians (cf. 1 John 1:5-10). Depending on when and where the phrase is used, "calling on the name of the Lord" can include: (1) obedience to the Gospel plan of salvation; (2) worshiping God; or (3) faithful service to the Lord. It is a figurative way of saying, "Do what God expects you to do." However, it is **never** used in the sense that all the alien sinner must do in order to be saved is to cry out and say, "Lord, Lord, save me." The professed Christian who teaches that all one must do to be saved is just say the sinner's prayer is in error.

Appendix B

HOLY SPIRIT BAPTISM

What is Holy Spirit baptism? The very first allusion to Holy Spirit baptism in the New Testament is John's statement, "I indeed baptize you with water unto repentance: but He who is coming after me...will **baptize** you with **the Holy Spirit**" (Matthew 3:11, emp. added). From this statement alone, one might be tempted to assume that Christians **in general** would be baptized in the Holy Spirit. But this assumption would be a premature conclusion. John was not addressing a Christian audience. He was speaking to Jews. Nothing in the context allows the interpreter to distinguish John's intended recipients of the promise of Holy Spirit baptism—whether all humans, all Jews, all Christians, or merely some of those in one or more of these categories. However, as is often the case in the Bible, the specific recipients of this promise are clarified in later passages.

Just before His ascension, Jesus told the apostles to wait in Jerusalem until they were "endued with power from on high" (Luke 24:49). In John chapters 14-16, Jesus made several specific promises to the apostles concerning the coming of the Spirit (the "Comforter" or "Helper") upon them, to empower them to do the peculiar work of an apostle (i.e., to recall the words Jesus had spoken to them, to speak and write by inspiration, and to launch the Christian religion). If these verses apply to all Christians, then all Christians ought to have been personally guided "into all the truth" (John 16:13), and thus would have absolutely no need of written Scripture (John 14:26). However, in context, these verses clearly refer to **the apostolic office**.

Jesus further clarified the application of Holy Spirit baptism when He told the apostles that the earlier statement made in Luke 24:49 applied to **them**, and would come to pass "not many days from now" (Acts 1:4-5). Jesus also stated that the "power" that they would receive would be from the Holy Spirit, which would enable them to witness to the world what they had experienced by being with Jesus (Acts 1:8). Notice very carefully that on this occasion Jesus made an explicit reference to the very statement that John had uttered previously in Matthew 3: "for John indeed baptized with water; but **you** [apostles—KB] shall be **baptized with the Holy Spirit** not many days hence" (Acts 1:5, emp. added). Jesus specifically and explicitly noted that the Holy Spirit bap-

Holy Spirit Baptism

tism He would administer (in keeping with John's prediction) would take place within a few days, and would be confined to the apostles.

All a person needs to do is turn the page to see the promise of Holy Spirit baptism achieve dramatic and climactic fulfillment in Acts 2 when the Spirit was poured out only upon the apostles. The antecedent of "they" in Acts 2:4 is "the apostles" in Acts 1:26. The apostles were the ones who spoke in tongues and taught the people. They were the recipients of the baptism of the Holy Spirit, as is evident from the following contextual indicators: (1) "are not all these that speak **Galileans**?" (2:7); (2) "Peter, standing up with **the eleven**" (2:14); (3) "they... said unto Peter and the rest of **the apostles**" (2:37); (4) Peter quoted Joel 2:28-32 and applied it to that occasion as proof that **the apostles** were not intoxicated; and (5) the text even states explicitly that the signs and wonders were "done through **the apostles**" (2:43). This pattern continues in the book of Acts: "And by the hands of **the apostles** were many signs and wonders wrought among the people" (5:12); "the Lord, who bare witness unto the word of his grace, granting signs and wonders to be done by **their hands**" (14:3); "what signs and wonders God had wrought...through **them**" (15:12).

The next direct reference to Holy Spirit baptism consisted of Peter describing the experience of the Gentiles in Acts 10. Referring to their empowerment to speak in tongues, Peter explicitly identified it as being comparable to the experience of the apostles in Acts 2. Note his explanation: "And as I began to speak, the Holy Spirit fell upon them, as upon **us** [apostles—KB] at the beginning. Then I remembered the word of the Lord, how He said, 'John indeed baptized with water; but you shall be baptized with the Holy Spirit.' If therefore God gave them the same gift as He gave **us** [apostles—KB]..." (Acts 11:15-17, emp. added). Peter unmistakably linked the baptism of the Holy Spirit predicted by John in Matthew 3:11, and applied by Jesus to the apostles in Acts 1:5, with the unique and exclusive bestowal of the same on the first Gentile candidates for salvation. If the baptism of the Holy Spirit had occurred between Acts 2 and Acts 10, why did Peter compare the Gentiles' experience with the experience of the **apostles**—rather than comparing it with many other Christians who allegedly would have received it during the intervening years? The answer lies in the fact that the baptism of the Holy Spirit did not occur during the intervening years. Baptism of the Holy Spirit was a unique and infrequent occurrence that came directly from deity.

Observe, then, that the first recipients of Holy Spirit baptism, as we have seen, were the **Jewish** apostles on the day of Pentecost in Acts 2. It equipped them to establish the church and to write, speak, and confirm inspired truth. The second recipients of Holy Spirit baptism were the **Gentile** members of the household of Cornelius in Acts 10. It convinced Jewish Christians that

Gentiles were fit prospects for the reception of the Gospel, and were valid candidates for entrance into the kingdom (Acts 10:34-35,45; 11:18). So Joel's prophecy, that God would pour out His Spirit on "all flesh," applied to the outpouring on **Jews** in Acts 2 and on **Gentiles** in Acts 10. The only other conceivable occurrence of Holy Spirit baptism would have been Paul, who would have received direct miraculous ability from God as well. His reception was obviously unique because (1) he was not an apostle when the Twelve received the Spirit, and (2) he was "one born out of due time" (1 Corinthians 15:8). Holy Spirit baptism, then, filled two unique and exclusive purposes: (1) to prepare the apostles for their apostolic (not Christian) roles; and (2) to provide divine demonstration that Gentiles were to be allowed to become Christians.

It should be noted that when Cornelius and his household received the baptism of the Holy Spirit, they were not immediately placed into the Kingdom of Christ. Peter announced immediately following their Holy Spirit baptism: "Can anyone forbid **water** that these should not be baptized who have received the Holy Spirit just as we have? And he commanded them to be baptized in the name of the Lord" (Acts 10:47-48, emp. added). One cannot appeal to Holy Spirit baptism today to take the place of water baptism. Verses such as Romans 6:3, Galatians 3:27, and 1 Peter 3:21 teach the necessity of water baptism, not Holy Spirit baptism.

Christ commanded His followers—after His death and ascension—to go into all the world and "make disciples of all the nations, baptizing them into the name of the Father and of the Son and of the Holy Spirit" (Matthew 28:18-20). That same command applies no less to Christians today.

During the early parts of the first century, we know there was more than one baptism in existence (e.g., John's baptism, Holy Spirit baptism, Christ's baptism, etc.). But by the time Paul wrote his epistle to the Christians who lived in Ephesus, **only one** of those baptisms remained. He stated specifically in Ephesians 4:4-5: "There is one body, and one Spirit, even as also ye were called in one hope of your calling; one Lord, one faith, **one baptism**." Which **one** baptism remained? One thing we know for certain: Christ never would give His disciples a command that they could not carry out.

The Scriptures, however, teach that Jesus administers baptism of the Holy Spirit (Matthew 3:11; Luke 3:15-17). Yet Christians were commanded to baptize those whom they taught, and who believed (John 3:16), repented of their sins (Luke 13:3), and confessed Christ as the Son of God (Matthew 10:32). It is clear, then, that the baptism commanded by Christ was not Holy Spirit baptism. If it were, Christ would be put in the position of having commanded His disciples to do something they could not do—baptize in the Holy Spirit. However, they **could** baptize in **water**, which is exactly what they did.

Holy Spirit Baptism

And that is exactly what we still are doing today. Baptism in the Holy Spirit no longer is available; only water baptism remains, and is the one true baptism commanded by Christ for salvation (Ephesians 4:4-5; Mark 16:16; Acts 2:38).

Today, every person who is immersed into Christ for the remission of his or her sins receives the Holy Spirit (see Acts 2:38; 1 John 3:24; Ephesians 1:13-14). However, that is not what the New Testament describes as Holy Spirit baptism, and it does not entail miraculous gifts given to each Christian. Instead, the Holy Spirit works in the Christian to produce the fruit of the Spirit which is "love, joy, peace, longsuffering, kindness, goodness, faithfulness, gentleness, self-control" (Galatians 5:22-23).

REFERENCES

American Heritage Dictionary of the English Language (2000), (Boston, MA: Houghton Mifflin), fourth edition.

Ascol, Donna (2001), "Everything a Baptist Mother Could Want," *Why I Am a Baptist*, ed. Tom Nettles and Russell Moore (Nashville, TN: Broadman & Holman).

Arndt, William, F.W. Gingrich, and Frederick Danker (1979), *A Greek-English Lexicon of the New Testament and Other Early Christian Literature* (Chicago, IL: University of Chicago Press), second revised edition.

Baptist Faith and Message (2000), Southern Baptist Convention (Nashville, TN: LifeWay Christian Resources).

Brown, J. Newton (1994), *A Baptist Church Manual* (Valley Forge, PA: Judson).

Davis, Andrew (2001), "When Our Senses Get in the Way: From Catholic Sacraments to Baptist Conviction," *Why I Am a Baptist*, ed. Tom Nettles and Russell Moore (Nashville, TN: Broadman & Holman).

Edgemon, Roy T. (1999), *Foundations of the Faith: The Doctrines Baptists Believe* (Nashville, TN: LifeWay).

Elliff, Tom (2001), "A Baptist on the Hot Seat," *Why I Am a Baptist*, ed. Tom Nettles and Russell Moore (Nashville, TN: Broadman & Holman).

George, Timothy and Denise, ed. (1999), *Baptist Confessions, Covenants, and Catechisms* (Nashville, TN: Broadman & Holman).

Graham, Billy (1996), *The Billy Graham Christian Worker's Handbook* (Minneapolis, MN: World Wide Publications).

Hobbs, Herschel (1964), *What Baptists Believe* (Nashville, TN: Broadman).

Hiscox, Edward T. (1903), *The Standard Manual for Baptist Churches* (Philadelphia: American Baptist Publication Society).

Hiscox, Edward T. (no date), *Principles and Practices for Baptist Churches* (Grand Rapids, MI: Kregel).

Malone, Fred (2001), "Misery Loves Company? A Presbyterian Pastor," *Why I Am a Baptist*, ed. Tom Nettles and Russell Moore (Nashville, TN: Broadman & Holman).

Mbewe, Conrad (2001), "Flying the Flags High in Africa: Baptist Hope for a Ravaged Continent," *Why I Am a Baptist*, ed. Tom Nettles and Russell Moore (Nashville, TN: Broadman & Holman).

McBeth, H. Leon (1990), *A Sourcebook for Baptist Heritage* (Nashville, TN: Broadman).

Mohler, R. Albert Jr. (2001), "Being Baptist Means Conviction," *Why I Am a Baptist*, ed. Tom Nettles and Russell Moore (Nashville, TN: Broadman & Holman).

References

Mosley, Ernest E. (1996), *Basics for Baptists* (Nashville, TN: LifeWay).

Norman, R. Stanton (2001a), *More Than Just a Name* (Nashville, TN: Broadman & Holman).

Norman, Stan (2001b), "Distinctively and Unashamedly Baptist," *Why I Am a Baptist*, ed. Tom Nettles and Russell Moore (Nashville, TN: Broadman & Holman).

Shank, Robert (1989), *Life in the Son: A Study of the Doctrine of Perseverance* (Minneapolis, MN: Bethany House).

Sullivan, James (1998), *Baptist Polity: As I See It* (Nashville, TN: Broadman & Holman).

Thayer, J.H. (1958 reprint), *A Greek-English Lexicon of the New Testament* (Edinburgh: T. & T. Clark).